VEGAN
ANIMAL HEROES SERIES

Guide to Save Animals & the Earth

Written by
SUSAN HARGREAVES

Illustrated by
CHOICE

Copyright © 2024 Susan Hargreaves

Publisher: Be an Animal Hero Press, a division of animalherokids.org

Veganza Animal Heroes Series: Guide to Save Animals & the Earth

ISBN 978-1-7357399-9-1 (paperback)
ISBN 979-8-9904893-0-1 (hardcover)
ISBN 979-8-9904893-9-4 (ebook)

Illustrated by Choice
Edited by Tanjah Karvonen
Layout and design by Kim Monteforte Book Design & Self-Publishing Services

Veganza Animal Heroes Rap written by Free Bison and Susan Hargreaves and performed by Free Bison

Note: Thank you to vegancalculator.com for the facts in this book.

A special thanks to: Sir Paul McCartney and Meat Free Monday (meatfreemondays.com); Maggie Baird and Support and Feed (supportandfeed.org); Tabay Atkins (tabayatkins.com); Gwenna Hunter and Vegans of LA (vegansofla.com); Dr. Jane Goodall (janegoodall.org); Angela Means and the Jackfruit Café (jackfruitcafe.com) and Heart Phoenix and the River Phoenix Center for Peacebuilding (centerforpeacebuilding.org).

Thank you to Suzy Amis Cameron, James Cameron, Suzanne McLure, Taylor Calloway and all of the staff and students at the all plant-based MUSE Global School for their enthusiasm for and collaboration with our mission.

Printed in the USA.

Veganza Animal Heroes Cast

Veganza: Susan Hargreaves
Freedom: Korin Sutton (bodyhdfitness.com)
Courage: Sky Bison
Wilder: Joaquin Phoenix
Free, vegan rapper: Free Bison

Did you know... pp. 26-29
Source: The Rainforest Book, Scott Lewis
Source: Vital Signs, Lester Brown et al., Worldwatch Institute, Washington
Source: Economic Research Service, USDA, World Agricultural Supply and Demand Estimates
Source: "Population, Resources, Environment," Paul and Anna Ehrlich

pp. 33, 35, 37, 41, 42 (top photo) photo credit: Igor Araujo
p. 42 actor in River the Cow costume: Finn Halecky, MUSE Global School
p. 42 MUSE Be an Animal Hero Awards, p. 55 superheroes in playground and back cover Veganza Animal Heroes at night photo credit: Nigel Duarte
p. 43 Sir Paul McCartney's Young Veg Advocate Award reprinted from *Animal Hero Kids - Voices for the Voiceless* book, p. 78
p. 48 fried rice photo credit: Alchemus Prime Wellness
p. 58 Joaquin Phoenix updates on Instagram

To Cherry & Freya,
Two Friends
who are kind. ♡
Veganzee

PRAISE FOR SUSAN HARGREAVES' EMPOWERING, ENGAGING WORK FOR OTHER ANIMALS NOT TO BE HARMED

"Susan Hargreaves' skill and ingenuity as a humane educator are vitally needed… It is precisely the type of outstanding educational programs and resources Susan creates that greatly benefits any community."

—Dr. Jane Goodall

"Animal Heroes Rock! The good news is we can all help animals in need."

—Sir Paul McCartney

"Susan Hargreaves' latest creation continues her decades-long work to engage the imagination and the heart to consider all species are interconnected. She understands our endless potential for adventure, magic and sanctuary.

—Ingrid Newkirk, founder of the largest animal rights group in the world, PETA

"I thank you, Susan, for all that you do in your community, for daring to innovate, for dreaming big, and for finding ways to create a better, kinder tomorrow."

—*Michelle Obama*

"How beautiful to equate the word "hero" with empathy and compassion for animals, qualities that children so naturally possess."

—*Maggie Baird,
Billie Eilish's mother*

"I was an **animal hero** at 3 years old when I felt that animals had the right to live free of harm and suffering. Susan's vital work to foster empathy and critical thinking leads to compassionate action, and ultimately, a more peaceful world for all."

—*Joaquin Phoenix*

"The world being a kinder place is what we're all about. Susan Hargreaves inspires all ages to be animal heroes. Her book is uplifting, empowering and exactly what the world needs right now."

—*Dave & Steve Flynn,
The Happy Pear*

OTHER BOOKS BY SUSAN HARGREAVES

VEGANZA ANIMAL HERO
A picture book (2020)

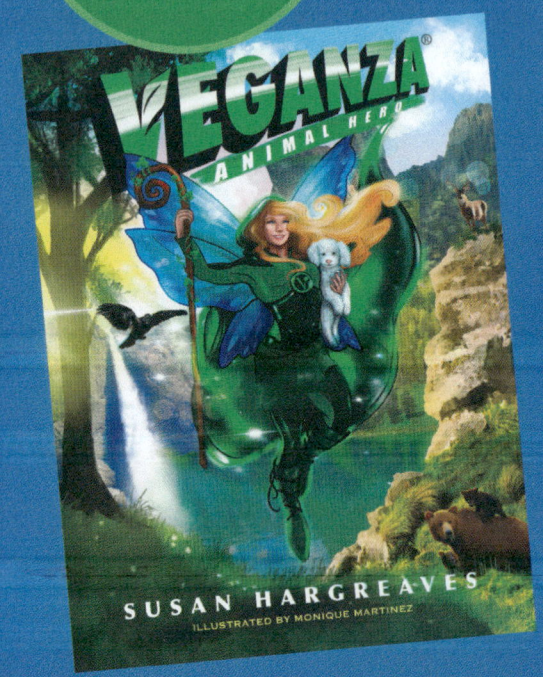

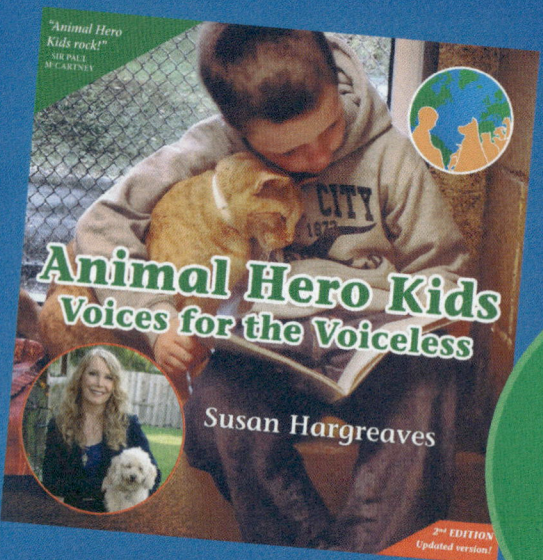

ANIMAL HERO KIDS
Voices for the Voiceless
(Volume 1, 2014 & Volume 2, 2019)

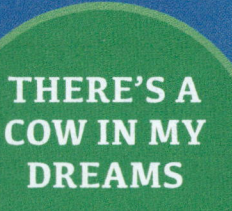

THERE'S A COW IN MY DREAMS
A picture book (2024)

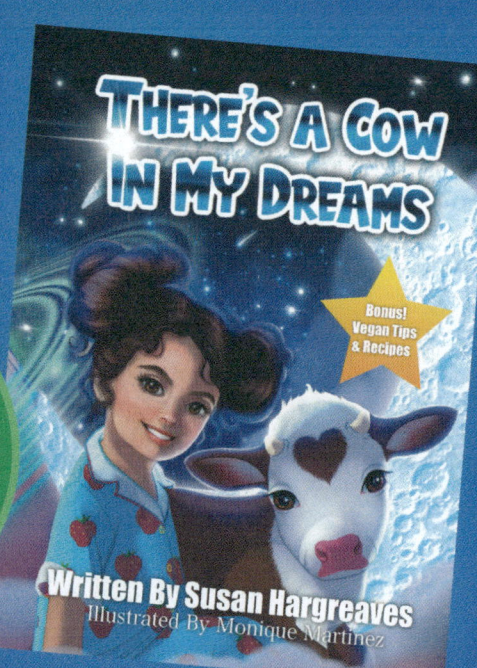

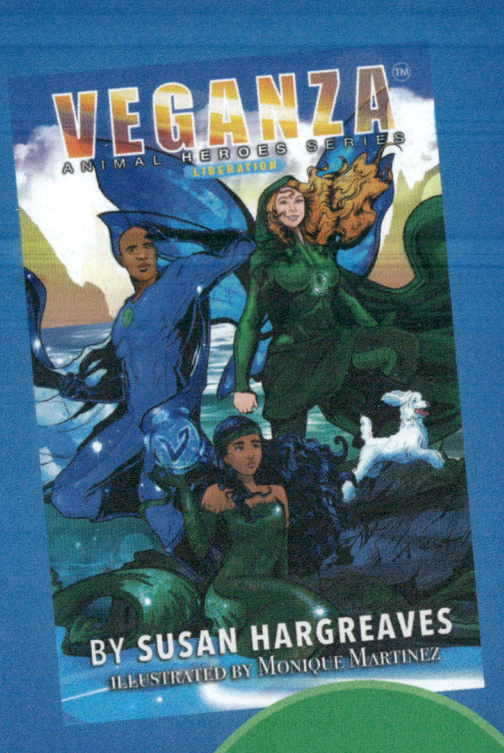

VEGANZA ANIMAL HEROES (SERIES)
Liberation
A graphic novel (2022)

FILMS INSPIRED BY SUSAN HARGREAVES

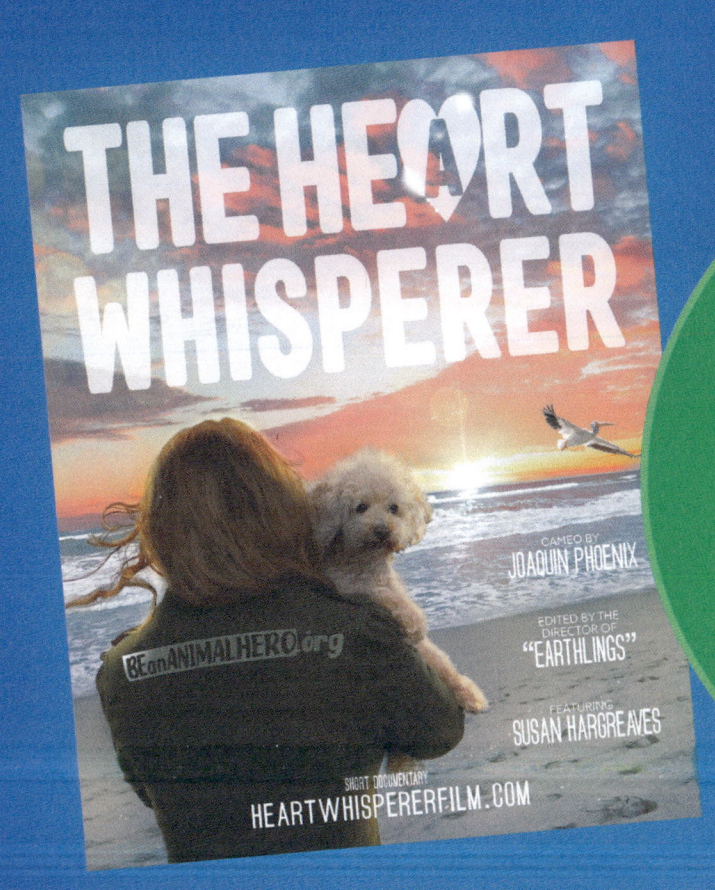

THE HEART WHISPERER
2023

One woman's pursuit to push the boundaries of our compassion

A new short documentary by Shaun Monson, the creator of the groundbreaking film, *Earthlings*, with a cameo by Joaquin Phoenix, features never before seen footage of wildlife releases and activism in action.

VEGANZA ANIMAL HERO CLAYMATION
2022

Starring: Angela Means, Gary Anthony Williams, Lori Alan, Tara Strong
Directed by: Wyatt Bergwin
Written and Created by: Susan Hargreaves
Executive Production: Chriss David & Associates
Animated by: Wyatt Bergwin, Bailey Magee, Maxwell Trullenque
Music by: Moby

A Claymation Short

Details on how to support, join, volunteer at BEanAnimalHero.org.

Help continue Susan's work empowering others to be animal heroes to all species.

*Veganza Animal Heroes Guide
to Save Animals & the Earth*
is dedicated to all those
individuals of any age who
are unafraid to act, to do,
to speak and to educate.
We are the answer.
You are the answer.
We are all heroes when
we choose plant power
over animal suffering.

Table of Contents

Introduction 3

Meet the Veganza Animal Heroes 4

Wild Horses in Danger 14

Why Vegan? 24

Did You Know… 26

How Vegan? 30

What I Eat in a Day by Veganza, Freedom, Courage, Wilder and Free 32

Epic Vegan Recipes by Sir Paul McCartney, Maggie Baird, Tabay Atkins, Gwenna Hunter, Dr. Jane Goodall and Angela Means 43

Word Definitions 49

Activist Guide 50

The Veganza Pledge 54

Veganza Animal Heroes Rap 55

INTRODUCTION

Welcome
ANIMAL & EARTH HERO
to Your Saving Animals and the Earth Challenge!

You're holding in your hands a guide to take the most effective step to help other animals, counteract climate change and aid human health.

Your mission, if you choose to accept it, is to join us in our quest to stop animal cruelty and to make the best choices for the planet.

The answer is in all of us!

Yours truly,

THE VEGANZA ANIMAL HEROES

Veganza  Freedom  Courage  Wilder

Meet the VEGANZA ANIMAL HEROES

Veganza

Veganza lives in a Florida Banyan tree with her rescued dog, Lovey.

She was born in the Wicklow mountains near the Irish sea.

The friendly crow reads the animal news from the trunk of the tree.

Then Veganza knows where she must be to make sure all wildlife stays free.

Her magic stick she waves and freezes scenes to stop cruelty.

The person knows to harm no more and lives life where compassion is key.

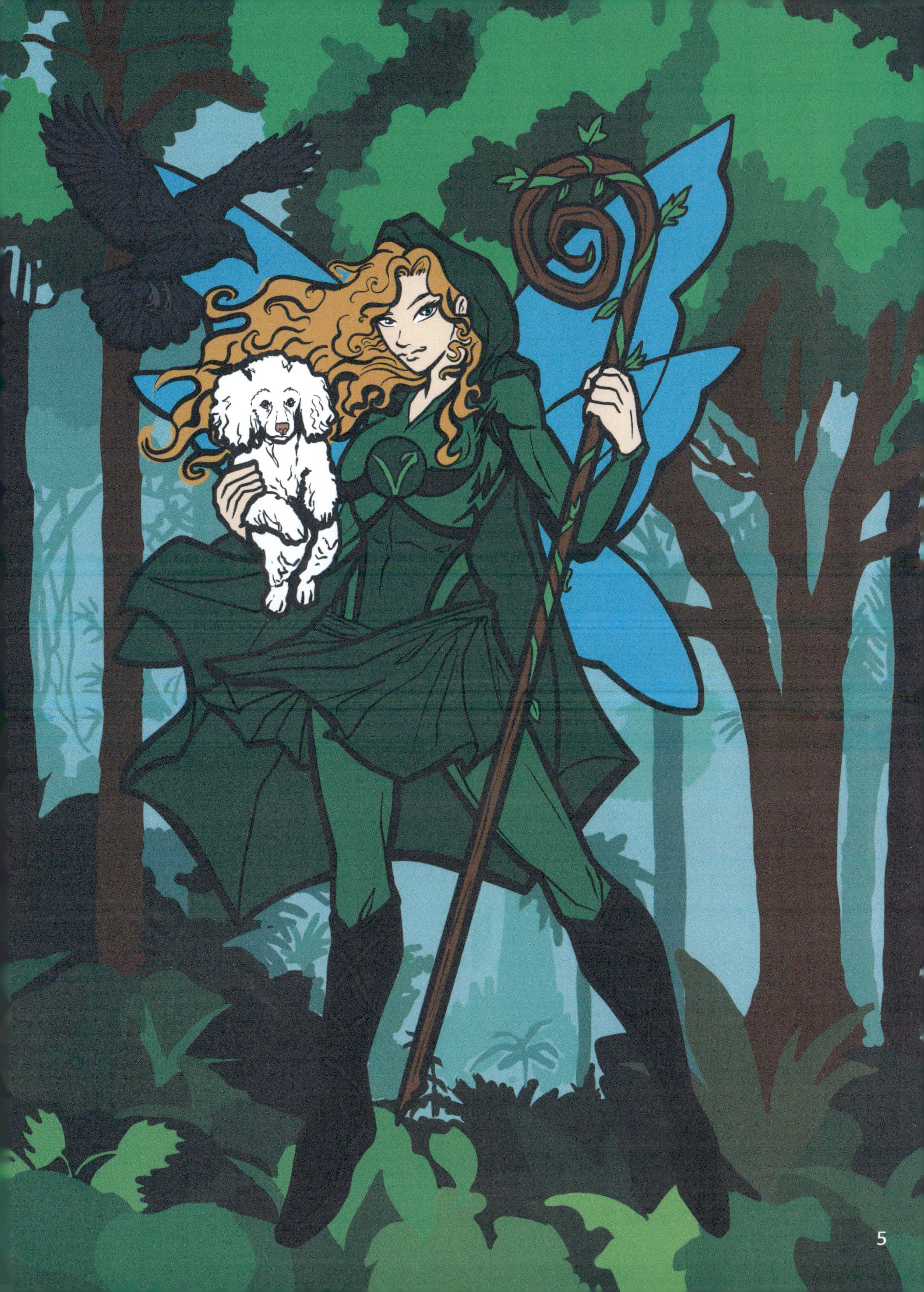

Meet the
VEGANZA
ANIMAL
HEROES

Freedom

Look up to the sky, is it a hero
or just a moving cloud?

A plant-powered hero with muscle,
let's say his name out loud.

It's Freedom, yay Freedom,
just say his name anywhere.

He wears a cloak of invisibility
and knows it's cool to care.

His superpower marshals all
the flying beings in the air.

Together, they keep animals free
from harm, everywhere.

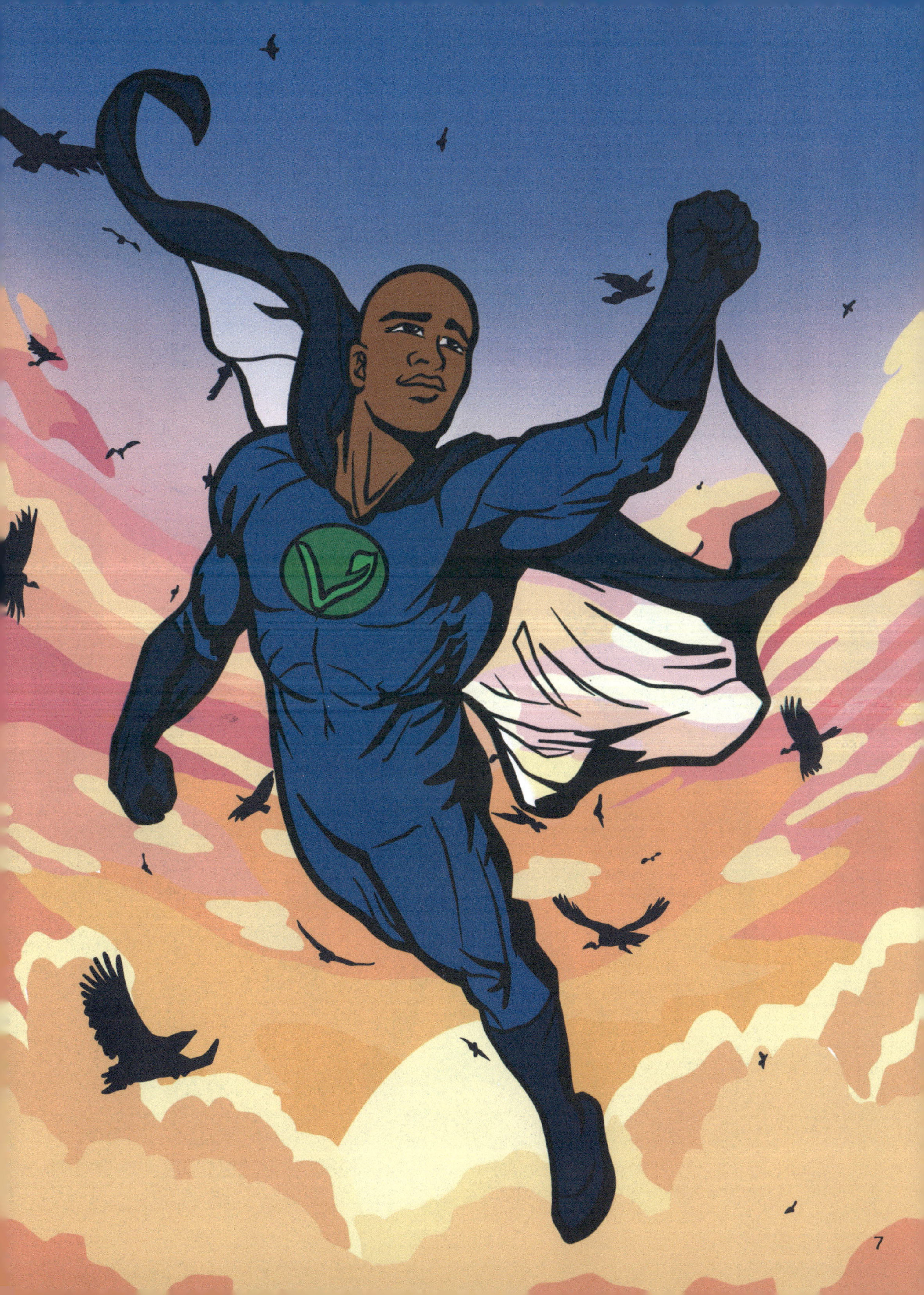

Meet the VEGANZA ANIMAL HEROES

Courage

Courage the mermaid was born under the waves, in a deep-sea cave.

She is super smart, her power is speed, and her spirit is brave.

Courage defends all her finned friends knowing alive and free is the only way to be.

She can make aquarium glass melt away and leads creatures back to the sea.

When she saves her swimming friends from deadly hooks and nets, her courage flows.

Courage is the ocean magic part of the Veganza Animal Heroes.

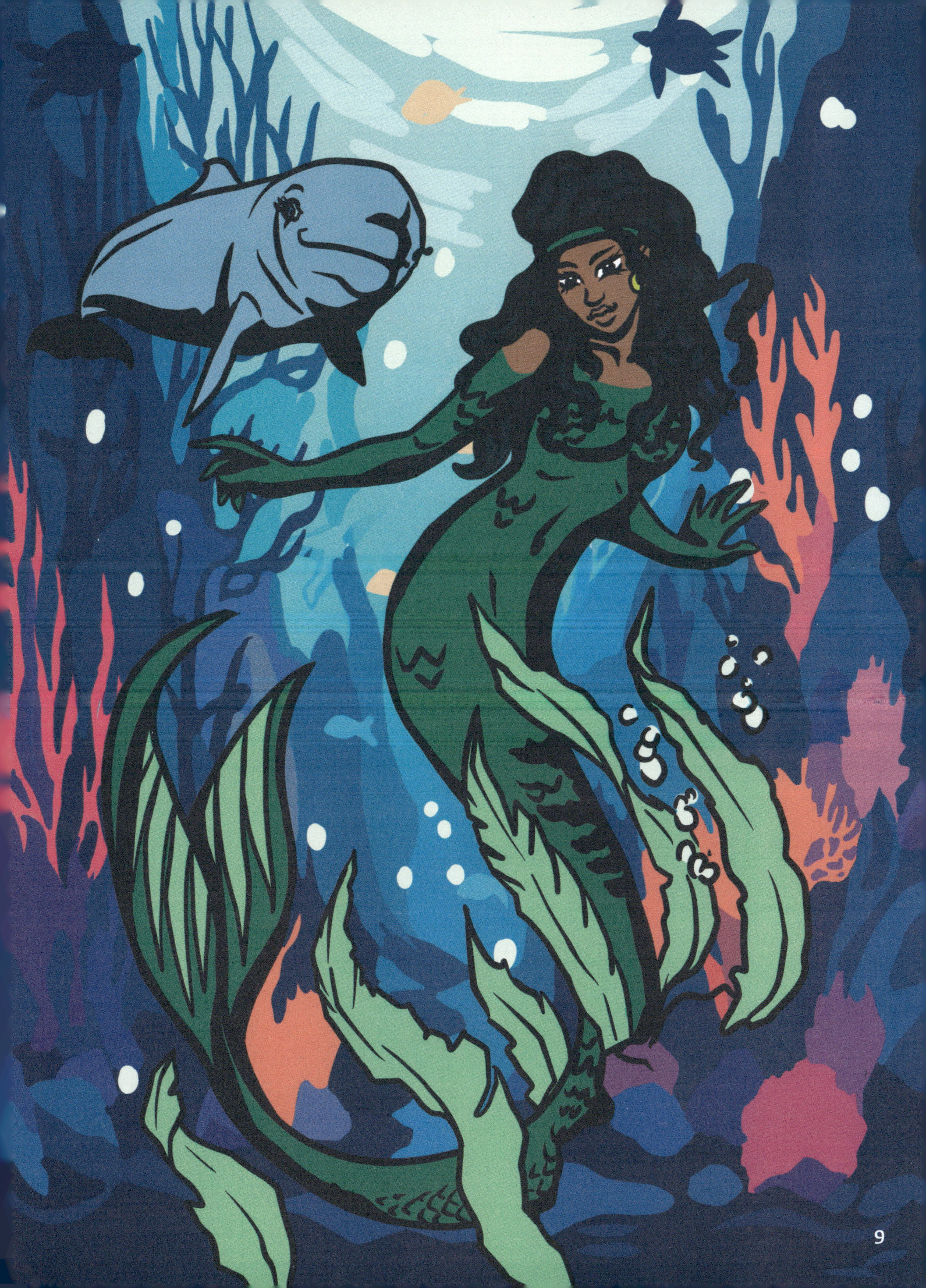

Meet the VEGANZA ANIMAL HEROES

Wilder

His earthly power grows plants, including trees.

We wouldn't have life on Earth if it wasn't for the birds and the bees.

His name is Wilder; he can travel through roots.

Quick as nature; wearing his vegan green boots.

Wilder makes forests appear when he raises his strong arm.

All the animals who live in the woods will come to no harm.

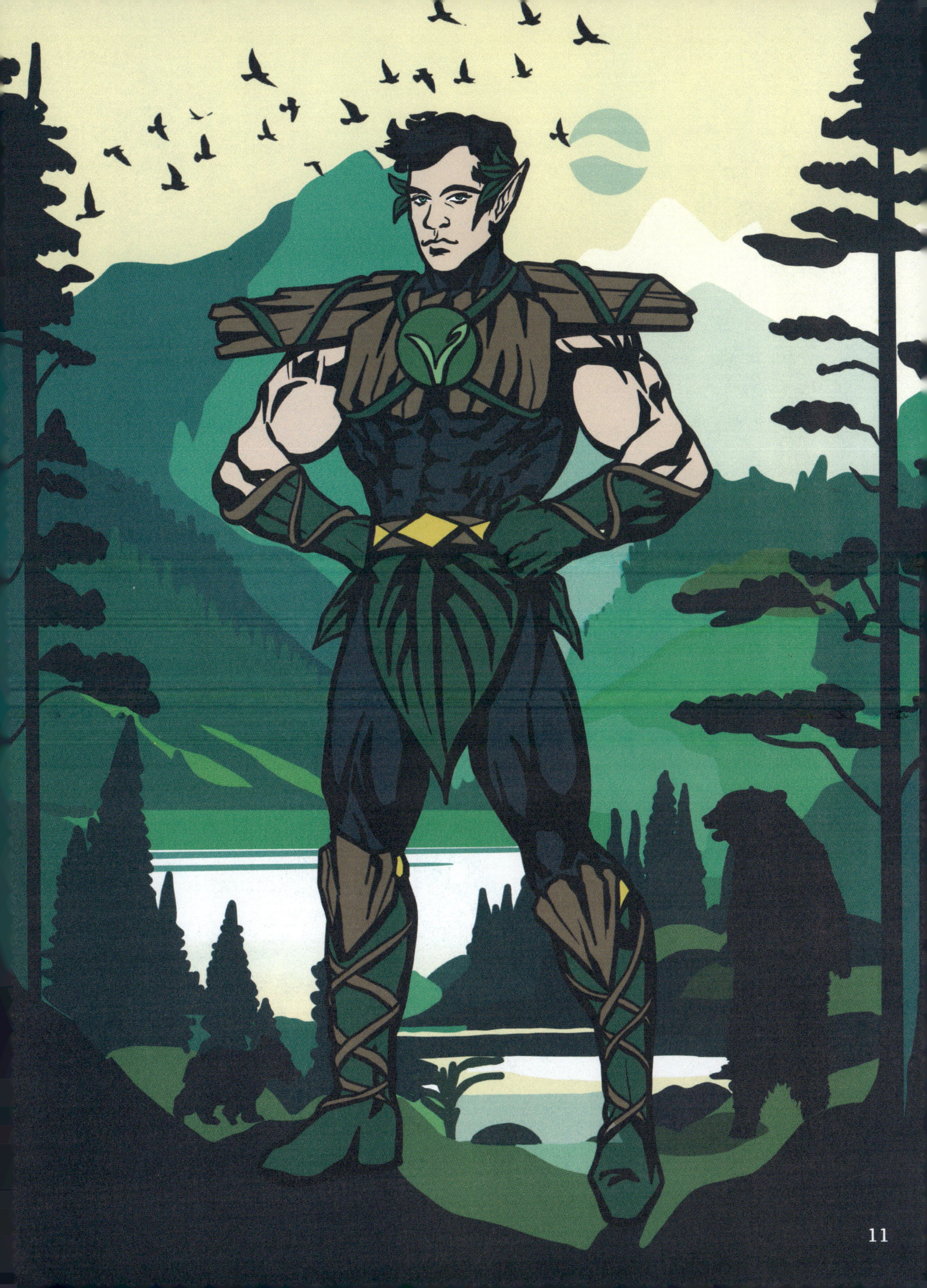

Meet the VEGANZA ANIMAL HEROES

Free Bison, the Vegan Rapper

This vegan rapping man helps the whole world, his name is Free.

His words open hearts and minds to how animals really want to be.

Free's music is his superpower, it circles the Earth, so everyone knows, to join the goals of the Veganza Animal Heroes.

Free Bison, the Vegan Rapper never lets any animal cruelty go by.

So be kind to all species of animals whether they walk, swim or fly.

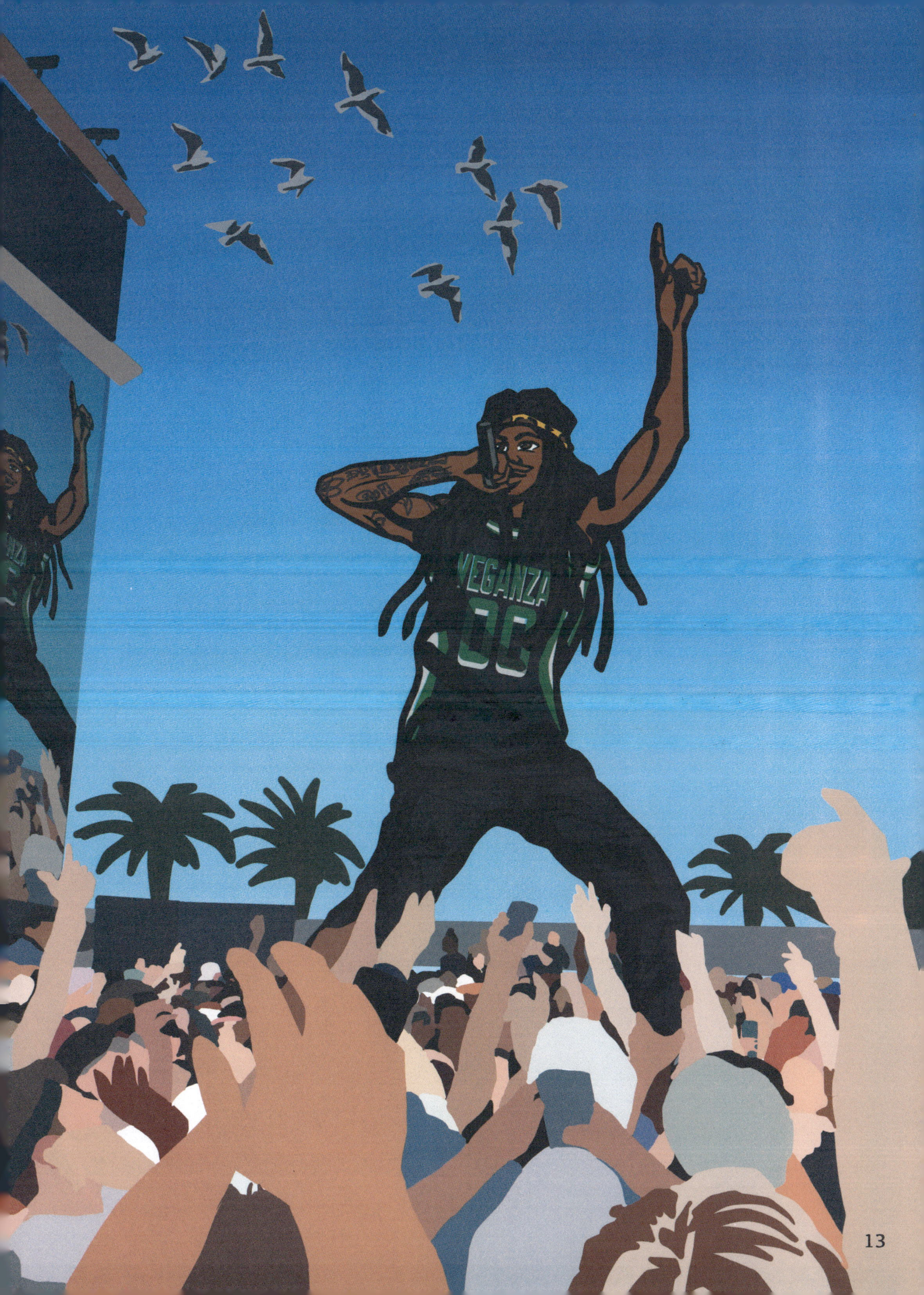
VEGANZA
00

WILD HORSES IN DANGER

The sun was coming up over the trees in Wyoming. Nestled in the valley a group of 30 wild horses gathered in a circle. Epona placed her soft muzzle on top of her daughter's head. "Smell the air, Hope, this is our land, where I was born and where your babies will be born, running free with the herd." The young horse with the fawn-colored mane whinnied softly into her mom's side.

Suddenly, a sound louder than any of the horses had heard before made Hope jump in the air. Epona said, "Keep close to my side," as they all ran, panicking, trying to escape the whirring of the helicopter blades. All 30 horses ran into a fenced corral as men quickly closed the gates.

"What's happening?" asked Hope, as her mom and the other horses all snorted through their noses in panic. "The farmers moved their cows onto our land and now we are in deep trouble," answered Epona.

Veganza raised her magic cane, a line of magic reached the two Bureau of Land Management guards and froze them. Freedom flew down to join Wilder and Veganza. The horses became alert. Veganza said, "When you wake you will know what it feels like to be chased, to be terrified, to be trapped. You will tell the world how wild horses are in danger and help stop the wild horse round ups."

Veganza whispered to the horses, "You will be free again."

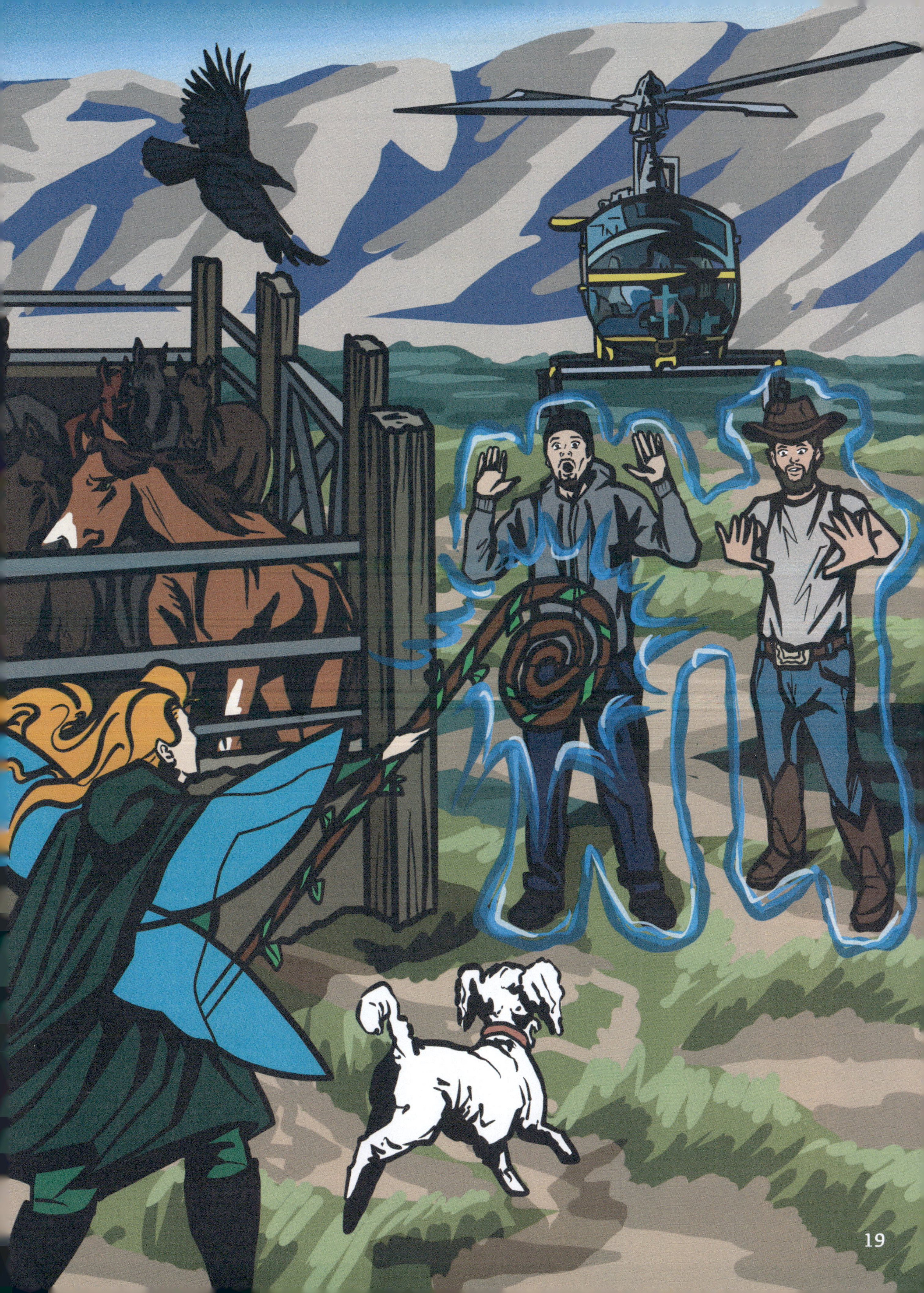

Wilder dismantled the fence. Freedom pushed down the top of the fence with his boots. Smash! The guards slept on, deep in a trance. "Hope, stay by me," whispered Epona. The horses all followed Veganza, Freedom and Wilder. They walked out of their prison and onto the waiting barge floating on the salt river.

The horses escaped to a part of the valley protected by Wilder, where forests would spring up when anyone meaning harm to animals stepped onto the land. When the guards woke up from Veganza's trance, they became whistleblowers, telling the world what really happens to wild horses, all because cattle farmers want cheap grazing land.

"Tonight, our special guests are Free Bison, the Vegan Rapper and Liberty, the band we all have grown to love with Pinkie, their rescued deaf pig friend, who tours with them.

When two whistleblowers, formerly with the Bureau of Land Management told the world what really happens to wild horses, the President made it illegal for anyone to capture, harass or even chase wild horses. Now, here's the new hit song "We Want to Be Free."

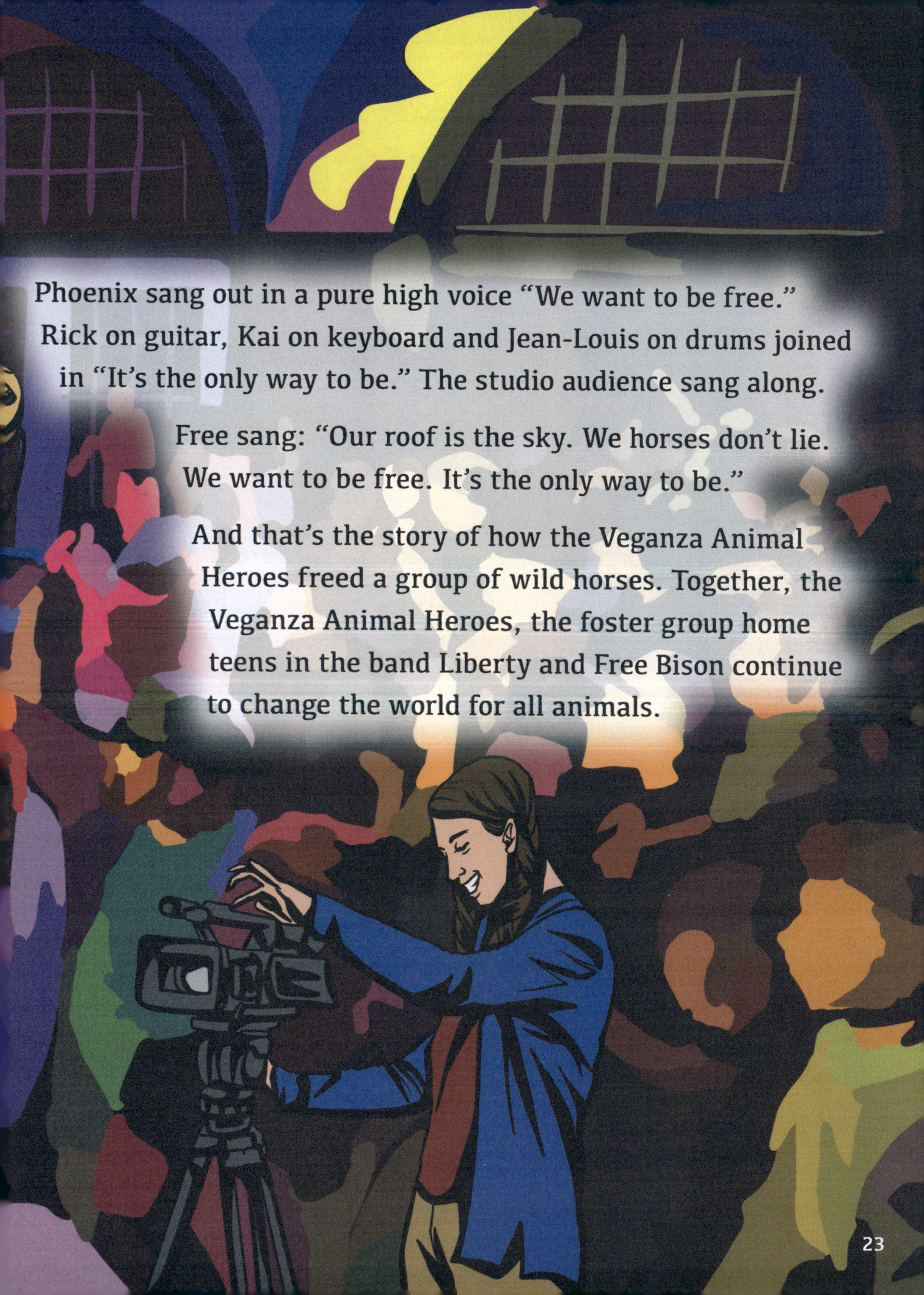

Phoenix sang out in a pure high voice "We want to be free." Rick on guitar, Kai on keyboard and Jean-Louis on drums joined in "It's the only way to be." The studio audience sang along.

Free sang: "Our roof is the sky. We horses don't lie. We want to be free. It's the only way to be."

And that's the story of how the Veganza Animal Heroes freed a group of wild horses. Together, the Veganza Animal Heroes, the foster group home teens in the band Liberty and Free Bison continue to change the world for all animals.

Why Vegan?

1. The Animals

So many animals are saved by going vegan; birds like chickens, turkeys and ducks and four-legged animals like cows, pigs, lambs, sheep and goats. If you eat vegan food and no animal products for one year, you can save up to 365 animals. This number does not include all the wildlife whose homes are destroyed for grazing land or to grow animal feed.

The Earth
2

Did you know that 45% of the land on the planet is either used as pasture for grazing farm animals or to grow grain to feed them. We can feed 8 times more people using the land to grow fruit, vegetables and grains. We can use less fresh water, less land and create less pollution by choosing to eat vegan.

Your Health
3

"Eat the rainbow" is a saying, which means if you eat plenty of green, orange, white, yellow vegetables and different colored fruits, it's like you are eating a rainbow. A good mix of veggies and fruits is full of healthy vitamins and minerals. For anything you can think of that's not vegan to eat today,
there is a vegan version.

Did You Know...

COWS

... cows can play games of ball with each other?

... cows take turns babysitting other mama cows' babies?

... cows form lasting friendships like we human animals do?

... the reason cows produce milk is the same reason human animals, raccoons and other mammal mothers produce milk: for their babies?

... humans are the only species who regularly drink milk from another mammal species?

CHICKENS

... mother hens talk to their babies before they hatch through the shell?

... chickens originally came from Africa, where they roosted in the lower branches of trees?

... one of chickens' favorite activities is taking dust baths?

... that today, on factory farms, chickens are so overcrowded they cannot even spread out their wings?

PIGS

... pigs can be good companion animals and can be taught to ask to go outside just like dogs?

... pigs have saved people from fire and gas leaks by waking up sleeping people and alerting them to danger?

... pigs have helped other pigs escape from a pen by piling up bales of hay for them to climb out?

... pigs make their own sunscreen by rolling around in mud to keep their sensitive skin from getting burned?

FISH

... puffer fish create works of art to impress a mate?

... fish can talk to each other using squeaks and squeals?

... half of all jellyfish can glow with different colored lights called bioluminescence?

... some fish help other fish by cleaning them?

... that in one year of eating vegan, you can save 365 animals?

... that 70 billon land animals and trillions of fish are killed each year?

... that every fact on this page about what cows, pigs and chickens naturally like to do they cannot do on factory farms?

... that 90% of animals are overcrowded on factory farms?

Did You Know...

EARTH

... the leading cause of wildlife extinction is farming animals?

... farming animals is also called animal agriculture?

... cattle ranching has destroyed more Central American rainforest than any other activity where wildlife lives?

... wild horses are rounded up and captured by the Bureau of Land Management in National Parks so cattle farmers can gain access to cheap grazing land?

... huge amounts of land, water and crops like soy, corn and wheat are used for animal agriculture?

... one half of the world's land mass is used for livestock grazing?

... seventy percent of grain grown in the United States is fed to farmed animals?

... that we can feed a lot more people by growing plants and using less land and water to make nutritious food with those crops?

... that on one acre of land, you can grow 20,000 pounds of apples, 30,000 pounds of carrots, 40,000 pounds of potatoes, 50,000 pounds of tomatoes or 250 pounds of meat from a cow?

... Harvard University, Oxford University and the United Nations all agree that farming animals has a very negative measurable impact on the planet.

Did You Know...

HEALTH

... these world-class athletes:

Venus Williams – tennis

Lewis Hamilton and Leilani Münter – racecar driving

Patrik Baboumian – weightlifting

Korin Sutton (Freedom) – bodybuilding

Chris Paul and Kyrie Irving – basketball

Carl Lewis and Morgan Mitchell – track & field (running)

Tia Blanco – surfing

Derrick Morgan – football

Hannah Teter – snowboarding

Vivian Kong Man Wai – fencing

and Prakriti Varshney – mountain climbing

... are all vegan?

The American Academy of Nutrition and Dietetics said "...vegan diets are healthful, nutritionally complete, and may provide health benefits in the prevention and treatment of certain diseases. These diets are appropriate for all stages of the life cycle, including pregnancy, lactation, infancy, childhood, adolescence, older adulthood, and for athletes." (Source: vegancalculator.com)

How Vegan?

Take a peek inside the author Susan Hargreaves' fridge and see all of the goodies!

- Plant-Based Sausage
- Frozen Fruit
- Plant Roast
- Oat Milk Ice Cream
- Cashew Cheesecake
- Plant-Based Meat
- Orange Juice
- Dairy-Free Cheese
- Maple Syrup
- Plant Mayo
- Vegan Dressing
- Soy Creamer
- Oat Creamer
- Vegan Scramble Mix

- Vegan Bacon
- Cashew Sour Cream
- Hummus
- Plant Butter
- Vegan Deli Slices
- Bell Peppers
- Oranges
- Watermelon
- Soy Milk
- Bread
- Tofu
- Spinach
- Broccoli
- Cabbage

Plant Sausage
Frozen Blueberries
VEG ROAST
Cheesecake
PLANT-BASED GROUNDS
WISE BACON
Plant-based
SOUR CREAM
HUMMUS
Veg Deli Slices
VEGAN SHREDS
Soy Milk
TOFU
TOFU
PLANT-MAYO
RANCH
SOY CREAMER
OAT
VEGAN EHGZ

What I Eat in a Day...

BY VEGANZA

Saving animals makes Lovey and I very hungry. Here's a day of healthy plant-based eating!

SCAN QR CODE FOR COOKING DEMOS

Breakfast

PORRIDGE

Ingredients:

½ cup organic oats
water
soy milk
cinnamon
vanilla extract

Instructions:

Cover oats in a pot by an inch (2.5 cm) with half water and half soy milk. Sprinkle the mixture with cinnamon. Add 1 teaspoon of vanilla extract. Slowly on low on the stove top cook the oats. Add a teaspoon of your jam of choice and fruit or nuts of choice.

Lunch

GRILLED CHEESE

Ingredients:

vegan butter
vegan mayo
vegan cream cheese
2 slices bread (thinner bread works best)
nutritional yeast
1 slice vegan cheddar
tomato, onion, green onion (optional)

Instructions:

Spread vegan butter and mayo on bread. Sprinkle nutritional yeast on two sides of the bread. Use a really good vegan cheddar slice for the middle. I also add a little vegan cream cheese on one side of the bread facing the cheddar. Some people like to add tomato and onion or green onion.

Pan fry with vegan butter on medium. When browned on one side, flip the sandwich.

Dinner

BATTERED TOFU

Ingredients:

¾ cup organic all-purpose flour
6 heaping tablespoons nutritional yeast
½ cup water (approximately)
1 teaspoon Savory Sage Seasonings
4-6 splashes Braggs Amino Acids
sprinkles of garlic powder
1 block extra firm tofu
enough olive oil to cover bottom of pan

Instructions:

Use two wide bowls - can be wide cereal bowls. In one bowl, add the flour, nutritional yeast and seasonings and water a bit at a time, stirring with a fork until the mixture is smooth (with the consistency of a smoothie).

In the other bowl, add the Braggs and nutritional yeast.

Squeeze the water out of the tofu. Slice it in half with a serrated knife and then cut pieces approximately ¾ inch thick from the two halves. Place the tofu in the Braggs bowl, then the batter bowl and drag it through, coating both sides. Transfer to pan when oil is hot, but not too hot. Flip the tofu with a spatula when one side is golden brown and place it on paper towel right after.

SAUTÉED KALE

Ingredients:

bunch of kale
olive oil
Braggs Amino Acids
nutritional yeast

Instructions:

Wash and sort or cut stems from kale and chop into bite size pieces. Once it is cooked it shrinks to a lot less kale.

Heat extra virgin olive oil on medium on the stove top in a frying pan.

A wooden spoon is useful for moving the kale around to ensure that it is evenly sautéed. Sprinkle with Braggs and nutritional yeast.

Both the tofu and the kale need your full attention on the pans. They can burn quickly or you may have to replenish the olive oil.

What I Eat in a Day ...

BY FREEDOM

My power and strength come from the plants I eat. My mighty muscles can lift transport trucks with animals on their way to where nobody wants to go and captive wildlife in cages. My feathered friends and other superhero friends help liberate animals. I must make sure my food is as plant powered as I am.

Breakfast

ACAI BOWL

Ingredients:

1 cup diced strawberries
1 cup blueberries
¾ cup vegan granola
1 frozen ripe banana
2 packages unsweetened acai
1 tablespoon coconut flakes
¼ cup plant milk of choice

Instructions:

Blend acai, sliced frozen banana and plant milk.

Empty blender into a bowl.

Add blueberries, granola and strawberries.

Sprinkle with coconut flakes. Enjoy!

Lunch

VEGAN EGG FRITTATA

Ingredients:

6 tablespoons Just Egg
1 cup chopped mushrooms
½ cup chopped bell pepper
15 tofurky slices, chopped
1 cup chopped onions
1 tablespoon minced raw garlic
approximately 3 tablespoons olive oil
salt
pepper
garlic powder

Instructions:

Warm oil in a cast iron skillet on medium heat. Sauté onions, bell peppers, garlic, mushrooms and chopped tofurky slices.

Add salt, pepper and garlic powder to taste.

Set your oven to broil. Add the Just Egg to the cast iron skillet and place the skillet under the broiler.

Dinner

FREEDOM MEXI BOWL

Ingredients:

1 8 ounce can black beans
7 ounces cubed extra firm tofu after squeezing liquid out
1 sliced avocado
1 cup cooked brown rice
¼ cup chopped onions
¼ cup chopped bell peppers
6 garlic cloves, finely chopped
3 tablespoons Bragg Amino Acids
olive oil

Instructions:

Coat a nonstick pan in olive oil and warm on medium heat.

Marinate the tofu in a shallow bowl with the amino acids.

Sauté the tofu in oil and add onions, garlic and peppers, then sauté all until light brown.

Set the pan aside. Heat up black beans in a separate pot.

Place all ingredients together.

Top with sliced avocado.

What I Eat in a Day…

BY COURAGE

Swimming, planning and liberating captive wildlife gives me an appetite. Here's my perfect day of eating delish dishes.

Breakfast

EASY 3-INGREDIENT VEGAN BANANA PANCAKES!

Ingredients:

3 cups rolled oats
2¼ cups unsweetened almond milk (or plant-based milk of choice)
2 medium ripe bananas
maple syrup (for topping pancakes at end)

Optional:
½-1 teaspoon cinnamon
¼ teaspoon vanilla extract
½ cup chocolate chips or blueberries or crushed nuts stirred in at end

Instructions:

Heat a non-stick pan on medium low.

Add all of your ingredients in the bowl and use a mixer to mix until smooth.

Measure a cup of the batter onto a pan. Cook the pancake until bubbles appear around the edges, then flip and cook until golden brown on both sides.

Move pancakes to a heat safe plate and top with your favorite add ons like sliced strawberries and bananas and maple syrup. Enjoy!

Makes about 4 pancakes.

Lunch

HEARTY LENTIL SOUP

Ingredients:

2 cups dry lentils
1 full container veggie broth (I use organic Pacific Foods veggie broth)
1 cup water
1 cup diced carrots
1 cup diced potatoes
1 cup celery
1 cup spinach
chopped onion and garlic (season to taste)

Instructions:

Soak the lentils overnight.

Remove from water and drain.

Cook them in boiling water with veggie broth until softened (about 30 minutes).

Add all veggies, let simmer and cook until vegetables are thoroughly cooked.

You can grab your favorite roll or vegan sourdough bread to dip into the soup!

Dinner

FRIED KING OYSTER MUSHROOMS, MASHED POTATOES AND GARLIC ASPARAGUS

Ingredients:

king oyster mushrooms

Batter:
oat milk
Just Egg
season to taste
flour

Mashed potatoes:
small bag red potatoes
vegan butter, heavy cream or soy milk
salt

Garlic asparagus:
2 bunches fresh asparagus
3 cloves fresh garlic
red pepper flakes
season to taste

Instructions:

Clean mushrooms. Mix batter ingredients. Dip mushrooms in batter, then in flour, then fry.

Peel red potatoes. Boil in half veggie broth/half water.

Season with salt to taste.

Mash with vegan butter and add vegan heavy cream or unsweetened soy milk.

Clean, rinse and dry asparagus.

Lay asparagus in a baking pan. Add garlic and red pepper flakes.

Bake at 350°F for 15-20 minutes.

What I Eat in a Day...

BY WILDER

Traveling through the roots of trees and making forests grow rapidly to block the way of people trying to catch or otherwise harm animals takes a lot of energy.

MAMA HEART'S TOFU SALAD

Ingredients:

1 container firm tofu
3 tablespoons vegenaise
Braggs Amino Acids
3 tablespoons nutritional yeast
3 stalks celery, diced
½ onion, diced
1 medium-sized carrot, shredded
½ head of lettuce, cut small
1 medium-sized Bubbies or other dill pickles to taste
½ tomato, diced

Heart Phoenix

Breakfast

I love avocado toast with lemon juice for breakfast.

Lunch

I often eat falafel for lunch with lemon tahini sauce, but there is nothing quite like my Mom's tofu salad (when I can get it!).

Have you guessed who Wilder is inspired by yet?

Thank you to **Joaquin Phoenix**, the real life vegan animal hero behind the new Veganza Animal Heroes crew character, Wilder.

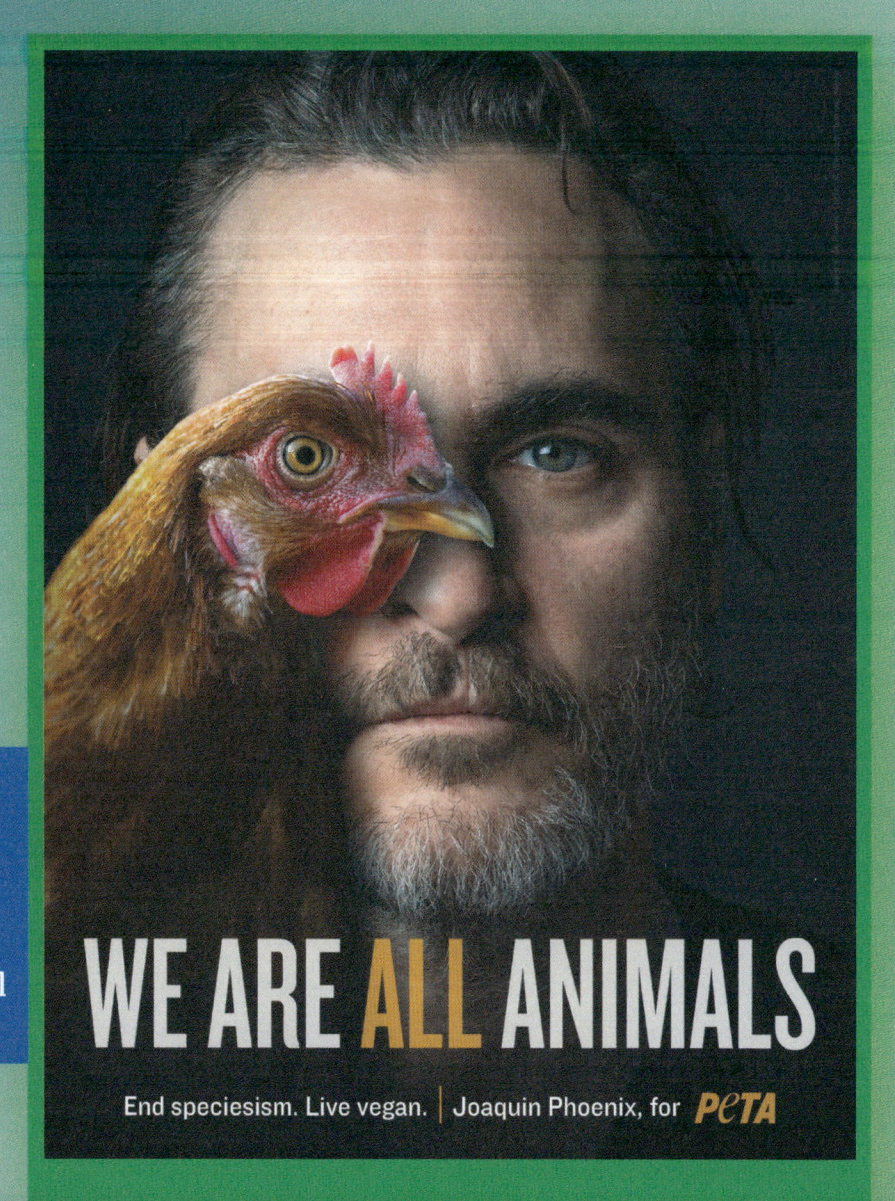

WE ARE ALL ANIMALS

End speciesism. Live vegan. | Joaquin Phoenix, for PETA

Instructions:

Mash the tofu and add each of the ingredients. If you need more mayo or Braggs, add it. Add crispy lettuce chopped small. (I use iceberg lettuce for this recipe only.)

Dinner

SMOKED PAPRIKA MAC AND CHEESE

Ingredients:

3 cups/340 g/12 ounces macaroni pasta (or pasta of choice)
1 onion, diced
2 cloves garlic, chopped
2 heaping tablespoons vegan cream cheese
½ cup/75 g raw cashews
1 teaspoon smoked paprika
1 teaspoon salt
½ teaspoon black pepper
3 tablespoons olive oil
½ cup/60 g breadcrumbs
3 tablespoons nutritional yeast
1 teaspoon garlic powder
potato mix
½ teaspoon onion flakes (optional)
½ cup parsley, finely chopped
¾ cup water
¾ cup unsweetened soy milk

Instructions:

Preheat the oven to 200°C (390°F).

Bring a pot of water to a boil and add the pasta. Cook as per packet instructions.

Drain the pasta once cooked and add it to the baking dish.

In the meantime, in a small saucepan on medium heat, add the oil, onion and garlic.

Place the cashews, nutritional yeast, smoked paprika, salt, pepper, water, the cooked onion, garlic, garlic powder and potato mix, plus 1½ cups/375 ml of equal parts water and unsweetened soy milk and vegan cream cheese into a blender, and blend until smooth.

Pour the sauce over the pasta, mixing well, and set aside.

Place in a cast iron skillet and bake at 375°F for 35 minutes.

Add breadcrumbs and toast for 5 minutes or until golden brown. Be careful as it can burn very quickly.

Garnish with parsley.

What I Eat in a Day …

BY VEGAN RAPPER, FREE BISON

Plant-powered fuel gives me the energy I need to create music and perform.

Breakfast

TOFU SCRAMBLE

Ingredients:

extra firm tofu
½ cup onion
½ cup green pepper
½ cup red pepper
⅓ cup garlic
1 bag of spinach
olive oil

Instructions:

Place large skillet on medium heat with olive oil.

Break up tofu into pieces, but not too small. Sauté until golden brown.

Add spinach and other vegetables. Sauté until golden brown.

Season to taste. Serve with avocado toast or vegan bagel.

LUNCH

SPINACH CURRY CHICKPEA WRAP

Ingredients:

spinach wraps
spinach
chickpeas
tomato
onion
mushrooms
ranch or vegan sauce
curry powder
olive oil

Instructions:

Cook chickpeas and season with curry powder to taste.

Thinly slice mushrooms and sauté until golden brown, then season to taste.

Dice onion and add to mushrooms.

Put spinach, chickpeas, mushrooms, diced tomato and diced onion into spinach wrap.

Toast in oven for 5 minutes.

Remove from oven and add ranch or vegan sauce of your choice.

Dinner

BROCCOLI & "CHEESE" SOUP

Ingredients:

3 cups vegetable broth
1 cup cashews
1 cup cashew milk
2 cups broccoli
1 cup chopped carrots
salt
pepper
nutritional yeast
paprika
onion powder
cumin
parsley

Instructions:

Blend 1 cup of cashews with 1 cup of cashew milk.

Add cashew blend to soup and boil broccoli and carrots until tender.

Season to taste with: salt, pepper, nutritional yeast, paprika, onion powder, cumin and parsley.

Serve in whole wheat bread bowl.

Veganza Animal Heroes with their delicious recipes and River the Cow, a character from Susan's recent book, *There's A Cow in My Dreams*.

Left to right: Korin Sutton, Sky Bison, Tabay Atkins, Sheree Johnson, Gwenna Hunter, Maggie Baird, Susan Hargreaves and, in front, the vegan rapper, Free Bison at the Be an Animal Hero Awards at MUSE Global School in Los Angeles.

EPIC Vegan Recipes

SIR PAUL McCARTNEY'S ALMOND SWEETS

CO-FOUNDER OF MEAT FREE MONDAY
meatfreemondays.com

Recipe taken from *The Meat Free Monday Cookbook*. Foreword by Paul, Mary and Stella McCartney. Published by Kyle Books. Photography by Tara Fisher. Find out more about Meat Free Monday at meatfreemondays.com.

Makes 30 balls.

Ingredients:

75 g stoned dates
75 g dried apricots
50 g seedless raisins
2 tbsp apple juice
50 g chopped almonds

Instructions:

Place 75 g stoned dates, 75 g dried apricots, 50 g seedless raisins and 2 tablespoons apple juice in a food-processor or blender and work together until smooth, scraping down the sides as necessary. Form the mixture into balls the size of a cherry, then roll them in 50 g chopped and browned almonds until completely coated.

Reprinted from *Animal Hero Kids - Voices for the Voiceless* book

"ANIMAL HERO KIDS ROCK!"

It doesn't matter how young or old you are, the good news is you can help animals in need."

- Sir Paul McCartney

Animal Hero Kids is proud to name

_____

As the recipient of the Paul McCartney Young Veg Advocate award for assisting farmed animals in crisis, human health, and the planet.

Your work helping the most abused group of animals on the planet is vital.

It takes courage and compassion to be a voice for the voiceless!

EPIC Vegan Recipes

Maggie Baird with daughter, Billie Eilish

MAGGIE BAIRD'S BUFFALO CAULIFLOWER

Maggie Baird/Instagram supportandfeed.org

Ingredients for Cauliflower:

½ large cauliflower, large even pieces
olive oil
½ cup plant milk
½ vegan bouillon cube
½ cup flour (including gluten-free)
salt and pepper to taste
½ teaspoons chili powder
½ teaspoon garlic powder
½ teaspoon onion powder
½ teaspoon parsley

Ingredients for Buffalo Sauce:

¼ cup melted salted vegan butter
¼ cup hot sauce of your choice
½ teaspoon rice wine or red wine vinegar
½ teaspoon garlic powder
maple syrup to taste
several grinds of pepper

Instructions:

Preheat oven to 400°F and add oil to a large baking sheet.

Break cauliflower into bite-size florets.

Add plant milk, bouillon, flour, chili powder, garlic powder, onion powder, parsley, pepper and salt to bowl and whisk together.

Add cauliflower to the batter mixture and stir until all pieces are evenly coated.

Use tongs or fork to pull pieces out of the batter and add to baking sheet.

Place baking sheet in oven to cook. Once brown on one side, flip the pieces and let cook on the other. Check periodically to make sure nothing burns.

While the cauliflower is cooking, prepare sauce: combine melted vegan butter, hot sauce, vinegar, garlic powder, and maple syrup in a bowl.

Once the cauliflower is done, remove from oven and add to serving bowl. Toss with a little salt and a sprinkle of pepper and coat with buffalo sauce!

TABAY ATKINS' SPINACH WAFFLES

tabayatkins.com

Instructions:

Combine the flour, baking powder, baking soda and flaxseed in a mixing bowl.

Blend the spinach, cashew milk, apple cider vinegar, vanilla and maple syrup in a high-speed blender.

Pour the spinach liquid into the dry mix mixing bowl. Mix together until fully incorporated.

Set your waffle iron to the desired setting. Once heated, pour an appropriate amount of waffle mix into the waffle iron.

Once ready, serve with maple syrup and assorted berries.

Equipment:
waffle iron
mixing bowl
high-speed blender

Ingredients:
2½ cups cashew milk
3-4 big handfuls of spinach
2½ tablespoons apple cider vinegar
2 teaspoons vanilla extract
3 tablespoons 100% pure maple syrup
2¼ cups all-purpose flour
(1:1 gluten free flour also works great in this recipe)
2 tablespoons ground flaxseed
2 teaspoons baking powder
1 teaspoon baking soda
assorted berries (strawberries, blueberries) and more maple syrup (for topping)

EPIC Vegan Recipes

GWENNA HUNTER'S VEGAN FUN FRIED RICE

vegansofla.com

Ingredients:

2 cups cooked rice (preferably cold)
2-3 shallots, finely chopped
3 scallions, chopped
1 yellow onion, diced
4 cloves garlic, minced
1-2 teaspoons cumin powder
1-2 cups shredded cabbage
your desired amount vegan protein (tofu, vegan shrimp, tempeh or seitan), diced
¼ cup cilantro, chopped
1-2 tablespoons ginger, minced
1-2 teaspoons thyme
1-2 cups finely chopped collard greens or chopped green beans or corn
1-2 cups mushrooms, sliced
2-4 tablespoons liquid amino acids
½ cup diced carrots
3 tablespoons sesame oil
2 tablespoons sesame seeds
½ cup chopped kimchi (adjust to taste)

Instructions:

Heat sesame oil in a large pan or wok over medium-high heat.

Add shallots, scallions, onion and garlic. Sauté until onions are translucent.

Stir in cumin powder and cook for another minute.

Add cabbage, vegan protein, ginger, thyme, collard greens and mushrooms. Cook until vegetables are slightly tender.

Stir in the cold cooked rice, breaking up any clumps. Cook for a few minutes until the rice is heated through.

Add liquid amino acids (or soy sauce), cilantro and chopped kimchi. Mix well and cook for an additional 2-3 minutes.

Sprinkle sesame seeds on top and stir to combine.

Serve your vegan fried rice hot, garnished with extra chopped scallions or cilantro if desired.

janegoodall.org

DR. JANE GOODALL'S CAULIFLOWER PUMPKIN SEED TACOS

Ingredients:

1 cup raw pumpkin seeds (pepitas)
2 cups cauliflower florets
2 Roma tomatoes, chopped
1 large jalapeño chili pepper, seeded
3 cloves garlic, chopped
1 tablespoon olive oil
½ teaspoon dried sage
½ teaspoon chipotle powder
1 tablespoon tamari
sea salt, to taste
8 corn tortillas
1 ripe avocado, pitted, peeled and cubed
juice of ½ a lime
hot sauce, for serving (optional)

Instructions:

In a food processor, process the pumpkin seeds until ground; scrape into a small bowl and set aside. Place the cauliflower, half of the tomatoes, the jalapeño, and garlic in the processor and pulse until minced.

In a large sauté pan, warm the oil over medium-high heat. Add the pumpkin seeds and cook, stirring, until lightly toasted, about 3 minutes.

Scrape the cauliflower mixture into the pan with the pumpkin seeds and cook, stirring often, until the mixture is soft and browned, about 8 minutes. Add the sage, chipotle powder, tamari, and ½ teaspoon salt and stir until the pan is dry, 1-2 minutes. Transfer to a bowl.

In another bowl, toss together the remaining tomatoes, avocado, lime juice, and a pinch of salt.

To warm the tortillas, wrap in a paper towel and microwave for 2 minutes, or warm each tortilla individually by placing in a cast-iron pan over medium heat, flipping every few seconds until hot, about 1 minute.

Divide the filling evenly among the tortillas and top with the avocado salsa and a drizzle of hot sauce, if so desired. Serve right away.

EPIC Vegan Recipes

ANGELA MEANS' COUNTRY CORNBREAD
FOUNDER OF THE JACKFRUIT CAFÉ

jackfruitcafe.com

Ingredients:

1¼ cups soy milk
2 teaspoons white vinegar
1¼ cups cornmeal (finer meal)
1 cup all-purpose flour
½ teaspoon baking soda
2 teaspoons baking powder
¾ teaspoon salt
1 egg replacer or Just Egg
¼ cup Miyoko's vegan butter
2 tablespoons raw sugar
3 tablespoons agave syrup
oil

Instructions:

Preheat oven to 400°F. Grease an 8 x 8-inch square baking pan with oil or butter. Mix the vegan milk and vinegar and let sit for about 3 minutes to create a buttermilk mixture. In a separate bowl, mix all the dry ingredients.

Slowly add remaining wet ingredients to buttermilk mixture and mix well.

Combine your wet ingredients with the dry and mix well. Your batter should be a bit thick but pourable.

Pour batter into your greased baking pan and smooth down with a spatula or large spoon. Bake for 23-25 minutes. Test by sticking a tester stick (a toothpick) in the center. The cornbread is ready if the toothpick comes out of the center clean.

Put the pan on a wire rack and cool for at least 10 minutes.

Serve warm with vegan butter. Excellent accompaniment for carrot ginger soup.

Word Definitions

barge: a flat-bottomed boat for carrying freight, typically on canals and rivers, either under its own power or towed by another vessel

corral: a pen for livestock, especially cattle or horses, on a farm or ranch

dismantling: taking apart piece by piece; snapping apart

fawn-colored: having the color of a fawn or baby deer; fawn is a light yellowish tan color. It is usually used in reference to clothing, soft furnishings and bedding, as well as to a dog or horse's coat color. It occurs in varying shades, ranging between pale tan to pale fawn to dark deer-red.

freedom: the freedom to be who you are; to fly if you are a bird; to swim in the sea if that's where you belong; the freedom to choose how you live your life, the state of having free will

grazing: horses, cows, sheep, goats, etc. eating grasses in grassland suitable for pasture

muzzle: the projecting part of the face, including the nose and mouth, of an animal such as a dog or a horse

nestled: settled or lying comfortably against something or someone

round up: the taxpayer-funded government act of utilizing low-flying helicopters to stampede and brutally tear North America's wild horses away from their native homes and chase them into lifelong confinement, resulting in thousands of wild horses and burros losing their freedom, and increasingly, their lives

vegan: someone who doesn't support animal cruelty in animal-based farming by not eating any animal products. They also don't wear animals, or support animal exploitation of any kind (e.g., going to a performing animal circus, going to zoos, wearing cosmetics tested on animals, etc.).

vegan superhero: someone who helps animals and the planet by not supporting destructive cruelty to animals. They choose to be kind to all animal species on Earth (including humans).

whinnied: (said of a horse) made a gentle, high-pitched neigh

whirring: (especially of a machine, like ceiling fan blades, helicopter blades or a bird's wings) making a low, continuous, regular sound

whistleblower: someone who blows the whistle on (alerts people to) what's really happening somewhere; it could be a company, the government or an individual who is doing something wrong, dangerous or cruel. This term comes from the idea that someone is alerting others by symbolically saying: "Over here!" while blowing a whistle.

ACTIVIST GUIDE

How to Start a School Club to Help Save Animals & the Earth

1. Decide what specific issues you want to focus on. Write a sentence stating what your goal is. Then answer the question about what you need to achieve success and make a list. For example, if you would like more animal and planet friendly food in your school cafeteria, do you need to start a petition?

2. Start talking to people about joining you, volunteering, have a sign-up sheet, or keep track of other students who wish to join you and how to contact them. If you can prove an interest from other students when it comes time to prove the club is warranted, that's great! Ask teachers who you know who may be sympathetic to animals to help. Some schools require a volunteer teacher to be a sponsor for a group.

3. Have your goal plan and proven support ready to present to your principal, dean or guidance counsellor when you ask them for an appointment to discuss your club idea. Every school is different. Be sure to arrive on time for your appointment with the knowledge that your goal is a lifesaving and vital one: helping animals & the Earth!

HOW TO ORGANIZE A PROTEST

Choose a place that makes sense to reach your target audience. Check where public property is. Precheck the property area for parking beforehand.

Depending on how old you are you may need your guardian's approval for the next step. Post your protest details on social media. Invite friends to share a message about why you are organizing the protest and why it's important they participate.

Write a news release with just the facts. Keep it short but include your contact information. Think about your answers to why you are protesting. Create a three-point sentence to give your reasons and make sure you include it in your answer to the media. For example, "Animal experimentation is cruel, outdated and wasteful."

Ask the news media to arrive 15 to 30 minutes after the start to ensure the protest is in full swing when they get there.

Create short, easy to understand chants. Borrow a megaphone to lead the group.

Get to the protest early. Thank everyone for being there. Lead the group by chanting with a megaphone. Try to keep everyone from spreading out too much so that it looks like more people/protesters.

Be sure to gather contact information from everyone. Send follow-up announcements and media releases with photos and videos.

What to Bring

Create leaflets, a banner and signs. Keep it simple to drive your point home.

HOW TO SPEAK TO LOCAL OR NATIONAL GOVERNMENT REPRESENTATIVES

Most city or county local government groups meet once a month and have time dedicated to public speaking on an issue they may need to focus on. Three minutes is normally the time limit. Practice what you are going to say and time it. When you arrive, sign up to speak. Be calm and speak properly in the mic. If you feel nervous, it's okay. Feel the pressure of the ground under your feet; it helps. It's okay to take a breath and slow down.

Dressing for success and looking polished and professional can help. Humans often decide whether to believe what you are about to say even before you open your mouth to speak.

Sometimes you can make an appointment to speak to county commissioners or city councilors in their offices. Be professional and polite when you do. Use facts/data to back up your opinions.

HOW TO CONTACT THE MEDIA

Write a short news release with the answers to the who, what, where, when, why and your contact information with a headline.

Email the news release at least one week before a news event and call the news station phone number between 9 am and 9:45 am. This is the best time for television news stations. Remember when you call to be brief and create a one sentence description. For example: "I am calling to ensure you know about the Veganza Animal Heroes who will be handing out free vegan food between 12-1 for animalherotober. I would also like to draw your attention to the billboard on the I-95."

Remember to keep it brief, polite and address it to someone's attention in the subject line. Create a one sentence sound bite which is a term for a short summarizing statement which drives the message home. For example: "We are in a planetary crisis. Animal-based agriculture is a key component in the destruction of our planet and cruelty to animals. We are here to prove how tasty a plant-based diet can be. Switching to a plant-based diet can help save the planet."

Today, a viral video has the capacity to reach more people than the traditional media does. Still, we need to use all methods of mass communication to get the message out to help save animals and the planet.

NEWS RELEASE

Contact: Susan Hargreaves
education@animalherokids.org

Miami Rapper and Veganza Animal Heroes Release Music Video for Animals & The Planet

Miami rapper Free Bison and the "Veganza Animal Heroes" characters from the book series of the same name join forces to help animals and the planet in a new original music video.

So far, the catchy --- and free --- music video has been viewed on Instagram almost 24,000 times. The goal of the video is to promote kindness to the planet and all its inhabitants.

"The world needs the Veganza Animal Heroes' positive, proactive and practical tips on being a superhero for animals right now," said author and educator Susan Hargreaves. "Music is the universal language and kindness is, too."

The video is produced by the non-profit organization Animal Hero Kids, which engages and encourages kids and adults of all ages to be heroes for animals.

The vegan rapper, Free Bison, and the plant-powered superhero characters visit schools in South Florida and around the world providing free programs as part of the Be an Animal Hero project.

Freedom is played by professional vegan bodybuilder Korin Sutton. Courage, the vegan mermaid, is played by Sky Bison, dancer, actress, and sister to Free Bison. Veganza is played by Susan Hargreaves, the Skipping Stone Honor Award-winning author of the Veganza book series and founder of Animal Hero Kids Inc.

The South Florida locals filmed part of the music video in Los Angeles at MUSE Global School, which was founded by filmmaker James Cameron and Suzy Amis Cameron. The school is the first all plant-based school in the United States.

The Veganza Animal Heroes can be booked for cooking demos of the vegan recipes from the adventure book series and to give vegan tips. Free programs, virtually and in person, can be booked through the education page on BEanAnimalHero.org. Free vegan tips can be seen here at www.animalherokids.org/vegan-tips-by-veganza/.

The VEGANZA Pledge

To protect ALL animals
and to help them live free from harm!

I _____ promise to speak up if an animal is being harmed and report the cruelty to the police and local humane society.

I will not participate in entertainment that jails wildlife, whether they swim, walk, or fly.

I realize that all animals deserve to live free from harm and stay in their natural habitats if they're wild. Animals should be cared for like family if they are companion or domesticated animals.

I will choose food that is cruelty-free and vegan where no animals are harmed for a snack or a meal.

I pledge to spread the word about being kind to all species of animals.

I promise to hold Veganza book reading activities, vegan treat eating parties where my friends and I can dress up as Veganza, the animal hero, Courage, the mermaid, Lovey, the dog or even Jules, the crow! You can even invent your own animal hero character!

We will create art, videos, write letters, and plan ways to speak to local government to help change the world, to make it a kinder place for ALL animals.

Do you know we have a rap music video?

You can see it on our website at BEanAnimalHero.org.

Can you write your own rap about saving animals and the Earth or a rap song about it being cool to be kind?

The Veganza Animal Heroes are not playing around with their goals of rescuing animals and saving the planet!

The Veganza Animal Heroes rap is a collaboration between Free Bison and Susan Hargreaves.

Veganza Animal Heroes

Veganza, Veganza
Yup it's Veganza
Veganza, Veganza, Veganza
Yup she's Veganza
And every animal crying out for help
She'll hear those
Cuz she's the animal hero
Veganza, Veganza, she's Veganza
Yup she's Veganza

Stopping everything cruel she sees
She knows evil is a disease
and empathy is her superpower
She's in tune with the trees and the flowers and the birds and the bees
and anything that breathes
She believes that animals ain't ours to eat, hurt or mistreat
It's time to save the day
but first she needs a team
and that's why she got Courage

Veganza, Veganza
Yup it's Veganza
Veganza, Veganza, Veganza
Yup she's Veganza
Veganza, Veganza, Veganza
Yup she's Veganza
any every animal crying out for help
They hear those
Now let me tell you bout the Animal Heroes

Courage that's what she feels
She defends her friends
with fins and gills
and she protects all seven seas
everything beneath it
(Wait)
Look up in the sky and you won't believe it
Is it a bird or a plane?
No his name's Freedom
He got a cape
and he fly high like a [an] eagle
to protect every nest with a bird's eye view
Animal Heroes you could be one too

Veganza, Veganza
Yup it's Veganza
Veganza, Veganza, Veganza
Yup she's Veganza

And every animal crying out for help
She'll hear those

Here's a Peek into Susan Hargreaves' Other Books

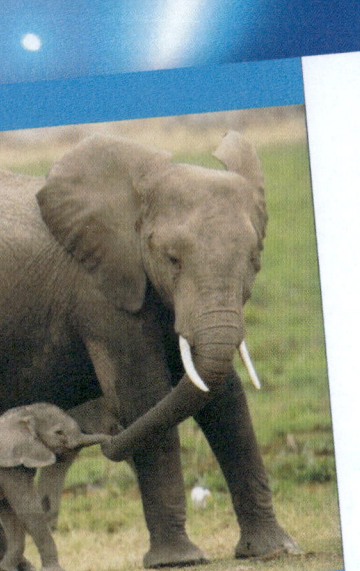

ANIMAL HERO KIDS
Voices for the Voiceless

This book features effective actions and true rescue and advocacy stories of animals in need. Susan Hargreaves' heartwarming stories of children and teens going above and beyond to help animals in need are astounding.

THERE'S A COW IN MY DREAMS

This is a delightful story about a courageous child, named Olivia and a young male cow, named River. Together, they begin a new adventure to change the world. Can two beings really make a big enough difference?

VEGANZA ANIMAL HERO

Veganza and her mermaid friend Courage are vegan superheroes with magical powers. They defend animals together and empower everyone to be heroes for ALL animals.

ABOUT THE AUTHOR

Susan Hargreaves is a Skipping Stones Honor award-winning author, a kindness educator, long time vegan, speaker and activist. She has rehabilitated wildlife and investigated animal cruelty in circuses, rodeos, aquariums and in the animal-based agriculture industry. Susan became active in the animal rights movement in 1980. She hosted the first animal rights radio series in both Canada and in the United States. Her relentless and lengthy journey to aid animals is the subject of a short documentary by the renowned *Earthlings* director, Shaun Monson, titled *The Heart Whisperer*.

Susan created the first interactive dramatizations in schools to create an understanding of the plight of other animals. She founded the youth-empowering charity BE an Animal Hero formerly known as Animal Hero Kids to prevent the animal cruelty she witnessed from an early age, by fostering empathy leading to informed, compassionate choices. Susan continues to collaborate with national and international organizations and is a regular speaker at universities, schools and conferences around the world.

Susan is a grassroots and global organizer at the frontlines of animal rights advocacy and protection. Her previous books are *Animal Hero Kids - Voices for the Voiceless*, Volume 1 and 2, and *Veganza Animal Hero -* a children's picture book, *Veganza Animal Heroes - Liberation* a graphic novel for teens and *There's A Cow in My Dreams*, a picture book for children. Susan is available for school assembly presentations and to speak at universities with *The Heart Whisperer film*.

Susan's work defending all species of animals has been featured in Yahoo News, MSN, National Public Radio, ABC, NBC, Hollywood Times, Dublin Live News, The Sun Sentinel, Deco Drive, MTV Music, The Globe and Mail, The Toronto Star and more. She is available for media appearances on the rise and evolution of veganism and its effect on climate change, empowerment to compassionate action, how to create change and all other animal protection and animal rights issues.

ABOUT THE ILLUSTRATOR

Choice uses his lifelong artistic ability to convey vital animal rights messages along with a sense of consistent justice. The environmental and health concerns caused by animal-based agriculture are also portrayed in the art Choice creates. Many pieces of his work have gone viral, viewed by millions on Instagram, being shared around the world by other vegan activists and organizations like Be an Animal Hero, a project of Animal Hero Kids and PETA. Choice was born in Brooklyn and raised in Miami and has painted wall murals in both cities. His latest illustrations in the *Veganza Animal Heroes Guide* add to his body of work aimed at animal, human and planetary protection.

The BE an Animal Hero Awards, which took place on October 26th, 2023 at the MUSE Global School after party at Crossroads Kitchen in Calabasas, California. Pictured from left to right: Tabay Atkins, Korin Sutton, Sky Bison, Karin Olsen, Alexi Wyatt, Free Bison and Susan Hargreaves.

Congratulations for completing the Veganza Guide to Save Animals and the Earth (if you haven't just flipped through the pages to the back of the book, that is).

We, the Veganza Animal Heroes, hope you will use your skills, initiative and voice to help save animals & the Earth. The knowledge gained from the Activist Guide segment of the book plus the Why Vegan?, How Vegan? and vegan recipes can serve as your vegan toolkit.

You can be an honorary Veganza Animal Hero with positive compassionate actions to be kind to ALL.

ONWARD!

Signed,

Veganza 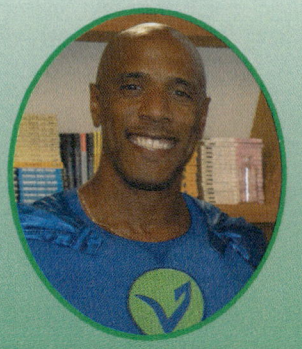 *Freedom* *Courage*  *Wilder*

Help us create
VEGANZA ANIMAL HEROES WORLD

The World's First
ANIMAL AND EARTH PROTECTION THEME PARK

VEGANZA
ANIMAL HEROES WORLD

1. Veganza Extravaganza Stage
2. Freedom's Sky Fly
3. Courage's Mermaid Slide
4. Wilder's Edible Garden

To help, contact veganzaanimalheroesworld.org.

To support, participate in or book any animal saving programs, or for a media interview, contact Susan Hargreaves at BEanAnimalHero.org.

Printed in Great Britain
by Amazon